Puss in Boots

by

Peter Webster

PUSS IN BOOTS
A pantomime in 2 acts

First Published in Great Britain in 2020 by Beercott Books.

Copyright: © Peter Webster 2020
ISBN: 978-1-9163953-1-2

Peter Webster has asserted his rights to be identified
as the author of this book.

Title is fully protected under copyright. All rights, including professional and amateur stage production, recitation, lecturing, public reading, motion picture, radio broadcasting, television and the rights of translation into foreign languages are strictly reserved.

A catalogue record of this book is available from the British Library.

No one shall make any changes to the play for the purpose of production. No part of this book may be reproduced, stored in a retrieval system, or transmitted in any form, by any means, now known or yet to be invented. This includes mechanical, electronic, photocopying, recording, videotaping, or otherwise, without the prior written permission of the publisher. No one shall upload this title, or part of this title, to social media websites.

Professional and amateur producers are hereby warned that title is subject to a licensing fee. Publication of this play does not imply availability for performance. Both amateurs and professionals considering a production are strongly advised to apply to the agent before starting rehearsals, advertising, or booking a theatre. A licence fee must be paid whether the title is presented for charity or gain and whether or not admission is charged.

Worldwide licence enquiries for this title should be directed to:
licensing@beercottbooks.co.uk.
Title subject to availability.

---

www.beercottbooks.co.uk

Beercott

CHARACTERS

JANE GRAIN – The Miller's wife
WAYNE GRAIN – Jane's eldest son
SHANE GRAIN – Jane's middle son
MICHAEL GRAIN – Jane's youngest son
TOM – The family cat
KING SEVIDENCE
QUEEN QUEASY
PRINCESS ROSE – Their daughter
SCAPEGRACE – An ogre
PERI – A good witch
MR BIB – A keeper of the King's wardrobe
MR TUCKER – Another keeper of the King's wardrobe
A LION
THE FARM FOREMAN
THE OGRE'S IMPS

Chorus of children and adults as villagers, rabbits, farm workers and courtiers.

SCENES

ACT ONE

SCENE ONE – Outside the mill (main stage)
SCENE TWO – A forbidding place (lower stage/half tabs)
SCENE THREE – Outside the mill (main stage)
SCENE FOUR – In the country (lower stage/half tabs)
SCENE FIVE – The Palace (main stage)
SCENE SIX – The mill kitchen (lower stage/half tabs)
SCENE SEVEN – The Palace (main stage)

ACT TWO

SCENE ONE – A forbidding place (lower stage/half tabs)
SCENE TWO – Outside the mill (main stage)
SCENE THREE – By the river (lower stage/half tabs)
SCENE FOUR – The Palace (main stage)
SCENE FIVE – The Palace (main stage)

ACT ONE – SCENE ONE

Overture of songs used during the show; some suggestions as to suitable placing of songs are made in the text, but directors are free to choose their own songs and to change their place in the action. As the overture ends, the curtains open to a scene set in front of a traditional mill. There is a large and obvious padlock on the mill door. On stage are JANE, WAYNE, SHANE, MICHAEL and a chorus of villagers. Some of the villagers carry sacks of grain to be milled. They go into a suitably upbeat opening number. As the song ends:

1ST CHORUS: (*Approaching JANE.*) Here, when are you going to open up the mill?

2ND CHORUS: We need you to grind our corn right now!

3RD CHORUS: Yes, we need our flour!

1ST CHORUS: No flour, no bread!

2ND CHORUS: No buns!

3RD CHORUS: No cakes!

ALL: And we're hungry!

JANE: Ever so sorry, but we can't open up, the lawyers won't let us.

WAYNE: Not until our dad's will gets read.

SHANE: Not until we know who owns the mill now.

WAYNE: Isn't it obvious? As the eldest, I should own it.

JANE: But you've got no idea how to grind decent flour.

MICHAEL: You were so bad at it that Dad used to call you the cereal killer.

SHANE: Don't annoy him, the last thing we need is a cross Grain. Anyway, I should own the mill – Dad promised it to me.

MICHAEL: Nonsense! You just made that up – there's not a grain of truth in that story.

JANE: Boys! Boys! All this worry is grinding me down. There's no use in guessing – we'll only know who owns the mill when we read that will.

1ST CHORUS: Well why don't you just get on and read it? What's stopping you?

MICHAEL: We just can't find the will, that's what.

JANE: No, no one knows where it is. We've searched high and low, hither and thither, under and over.

MICHAEL: Up and down, front and back – not a sign.

2ND CHORUS: Have you looked under the bed?

3RD CHORUS: Have you looked in that drawer in the kitchen where you put everything you can't find a home for?

1ST CHORUS: Have you looked in the washing tub?

JANE: Certainly not! I'm not airing my dirty linen in public.

MICHAEL: Yes! Yes! Yes! We've looked everywhere. No sign of it.

1ST CHORUS: Well you'd better hurry up and find it and open up the mill.

2ND CHORUS: Otherwise we'll just have to take our business elsewhere.

3RD CHORUS: So you'd better put your noses to the grindstone.

JANE: What? Take your business elsewhere? That really goes against the grain.

1ST CHORUS: Tough luck! You've got one more day. We'll be back tomorrow and if the mill isn't open then, you know what'll happen.

ALL: You'll be toast! (*The chorus exit grumbling.*)

MICHAEL: Well what do you suggest we do now? (*THE GRAINS all make gestures of helplessness as the curtains close.*)

Scene Two

> *The lighting changes to a dim green; wisps of smoke move over the floor. There are occasional flashes of lightning and the sound of distant thunder.* THE IMPS *precede the* OGRE *onto the lower stage or in front of half tabs, bowing and scraping as they go.*

1ST IMP: This way sir.

2ND IMP: We'll clear the path.

3RD IMP: Nothing will bar your progress.

4TH IMP: We'll see to that.

OGRE: Indeed you will! And what's all this 'sir' business? You can do better than that, surely? (*Smoothly and reasonably.*) Shall we try again? Humour me.

1ST IMP: Of course, your eminence!

2ND IMP: Your magnificence!

3RD IMP: Your splendidness!

4TH IMP: Your highness!

OGRE: That's better – but don't get too carried away; just remember your manners next time – otherwise there may not be a next time! Now – today's team meeting; is everybody here?

IMPS: Yes, your greatness!

OGRE: Good. Now my imps, what are you going to bring me today? What more treasures do you have for me?

2ND IMP: That could be a teeny, weeny problem master.

OGRE: (*Angry now.*) Problem? Problem? Explain!

3RD IMP: Well, it's like this…..

1ST IMP: Every day we go out to look for treasure to fill your vaults…..

4TH IMP: And every day we bring something back.

OGRE: Yes – and so? As I said, what's your problem?

1ST IMP: (*Quietly.*) There's no treasure left.

OGRE: What did you say? Speak up!

1ST IMP: (*Louder.*) I said – there's no treasure left.

2ND IMP: We've taken everything worth taking....

4TH IMP: And now it's all in your vaults......

3RD IMP: All the gold, silver, jewels, pictures, hangings, money – you've got the lot!

OGRE: Oh dear, oh dear – that is a problem; for you, not for me. Well team, what do you suggest? Because suggest you must!

4TH IMP: Perhaps it's time to take over another kingdom?

2ND IMP: More lands, more people, more treasures!

3RD IMP: And lots more opportunities to be your true heartless self!

1ST IMP: You already have all the kingdoms to the north, the east and the west; that still leaves the lands over the river to the south.

4TH IMP: But we never go south of the river!

2ND IMP: It's a cultural desert.

3RD IMP: And you can never get a sedan chair to take you there.

OGRE: Now, now boys, don't be so parochial. I like the idea; we go to the south. What do we do?

IMPS: (*In unison.*) We go to the south!

OGRE: We need to be prepared; so, let's see who and what is there for us. Fetch me my seeing bowl!

IMPS: Yes master! At once, master!

One of the imps goes offstage and returns with a large, beautifully decorated bowl. He kneels in front of the OGRE and holds up the bowl. The OGRE appears to stir the 'water' in the bowl and peers intently into it. More smoke, lightning and distant thunder.

OGRE: What's this I see? *(He stirs the bowl once more.)* A splendid palace, a decorated hall; there are people in it – I see a king, a queen, many courtiers and – a princess! How <u>very</u> interesting. I see jewels and fine clothes, rich pickings indeed. I also see decadence and weakness – a kingdom ripe for the taking. I'll take that palace and all their possessions and lands. And while I'm at it, I may as well steal away that princess as well. Oh, this is more like it! A challenge at last, just like the old days! Time for one of my cunning plans. *(He turns to his IMPS.)* Well, what do you think? Am I not a genius and a despot of the first order?

IMPS: Indeed you are, master!

OGRE: In fact, I'm so pleased with myself that I feel like singing. *(To the IMPS.)* And you lot can join in too. *(To the audience.)* And you will enjoy yourselves – or else!

Song: possibly 'Perfect', Fairground attraction – the OGRE and the IMPS. As the song ends, he turns to the imps.

OGRE: I hope you're impressed!

IMPS: *(With more bowing and scraping.)* We are, master, we are! Very impressed!

OGRE: Lucky for you then; a lack of enthusiasm could be bad for your health! Now, back to work all of you – there are plans to make and lands to seize. *(He exits, followed by the IMPS.)*

IMPS: *(As they go.)* Plans to make and lands to seize!

Scene Three

Outside the mill. On stage are MICHAEL, JANE, WAYNE and SHANE, together with the chorus of villagers, some of whom are carrying their sacks of grain. There is a basket to one side with a CAT in it, apparently fast asleep. JANE is holding a very large and impressive legal document, peering through very large thick glasses and turning it over and over, while WAYNE and SHANE are looking over her shoulder. The padlock has been removed from the mill door.

1ST CHORUS: You found it then?

2ND CHORUS: Your old dad's will.

3RD CHORUS: So where was it hidden?

JANE: Those rotten lawyers had it all the time.

WAYNE: They said they were keeping it warm for us....

SHANE: But they wouldn't hand it over....

MICHAEL: Till we could prove we were the rightful heirs.

2ND CHORUS: How did you do that, then?

MICHAEL: Easy; all we had to do was promise them a year's supply of free flour. Oh, that and get down on our bended knees.

JANE: That really took the wind out of our sails. Get it? Windmill? Sails?

MICHAEL: Oh, Mum – that's really corny!

JANE: Well it's all grist to the mill.

3RD CHORUS: When you've quite finished....

1ST CHORUS: Are you going to grind our corn or not?

WAYNE: Of course we are.

SHANE: Put it here. *(He indicates a space by the mill door. The villagers place their sacks there.)*

2ND CHORUS: Seeing as you've kept us waiting for our flour, the least you can do is read that will.

Act 1　　　　　　　　PUSS IN BOOTS　　　　　　　　11

3RD CHORUS: Yes, we want to know who owns the mill.

1ST CHORUS: Not that we're nosey or anything.

JANE: Oh, very well. Now, let's see…. *(Again she peers intently at the document.)* I can't make head or tail of this.

MICHAEL: *(Taking the document, turning it over and returning it to her.)* I'm not surprised – you've got it upside down.

WAYNE: Let me see it then.

SHANE: No, me first!

JANE: You must both wait your turn, while I try and make sense of all this legal loopiness.

WAYNE: Knowing you, mother, that will take all day.

SHANE: And half the night; you're so slow.

MICHAEL: Leave her alone you two, mum's doing her best.

WAYNE: Shut up, Mi!

MICHAEL: I wish you wouldn't call me that.

JANE: And I wish you wouldn't call your little brother Mi. Why do you do it? It's horrible.

SHANE: So's he; it's short for migraine.

WAYNE: Because he's such a pain in the…… *(The chorus laugh at this.)*

JANE: That's enough! Will you two go away and let me read this in peace. Your poor Dad; he's hardly shuffled off his mortal coil and *(To WAYNE and SHANE.)* all you two can think about is what he might have left you.

MICHAEL: Well they would; greedy so-and-sos.

SHANE: We want our just desserts.

JANE: If you carry on this way, believe me you'll get 'em. I can still give you a good slapping. *(She tries to shake herself free; WAYNE and SHANE both try to grab the document which is dropped in the unseemly struggle, allowing MICHAEL to pick it up.)*

MICHAEL: Here, let me read it! Probably just as well, as I'm the only one who <u>can</u> read.

WAYNE: I can't be bothered with all that reading lark, nor sums.

SHANE: Just because you're the only one who could be bothered to get up early enough to go to school. Rotten little swot! Give me bed before books any day.

JANE: Don't we know it. How will you two ever do the mill books, without an ounce of education, I'd like to know.

WAYNE: Simple. We'll do what dad did – we'll rely on our culinary skills.

MICHAEL: What on earth does that mean?

SHANE: We'll cook them!

MICHAEL: Do you want to know what's in this here will or not?

ALL: Yes!

MICHAEL: Then listen! *(Reading.)* To my eldest son, Wayne, I leave the mill and all its contents. *(The chorus applaud.)*

WAYNE: *(Jumping up and down.)* Goody, I'm rich! Rich! Rich!

MICHAEL: When you've quite finished gloating, can I get on? "To my son Shane, I leave all the horses and carts. It is my intention that Wayne and Shane must depend on each other for their living; they will never get on any other way." *(Again, the chorus applaud.)*

JANE: True, so true!

SHANE: *(To WAYNE.)* There, see! You can't do without me! No horse, no cart – no grain. No grain, no flour – no money!

WAYNE: It looks as if I'm stuck with you and you with me. But what does that leave you, little brother?

MICHAEL: *(Reading on. A long pause.)* It seems that I get the cat and have to look after mum. *(The chorus fall about laughing.)*

JANE: I was wondering when I'd come into all this.

WAYNE: He gets the cat, that's all! What a joke!

SHANE: Lost out by a whisker!

JANE: You mean there's nothing left in the kitty?

The chorus begin to drift offstage, with comments such as "He's got the cat, what a joke", "Here puss, nice puss", "what a turn up", " now, don't let's be catty" etc.

MICHAEL: It's not funny, mum. I'm going to challenge this will, I am. I want a lawyer!

ALL: Oh no, you don't!

MICHAEL: Oh yes, I do!

JANE: We've dealt with lawyers before and look how much good it's done us. You know the only ones in town are Shyster, Fiddle and Fudgit and they're more crooked than these two.

WAYNE: By the time we've paid their fees......

SHANE: There'd be nothing left for us.

MICHAEL: It's alright for you – I'm stuck with that useless animal. *(Indicating the basket.)* It may be good at catching mice and rats, but that's all it's good for! Lazy layabout furball! *(PERI enters without warning, making JANE jump.)*

JANE: Ooh! Er! Where did you spring from? Why can't you announce your presence, like normal people?

PERI: Sorry, but that's the way us witches work – by stealth. We fly in under the radar, so no one knows we're there.

WAYNE: Why do you keep turning up anyway? You're not wanted you know.

SHANE: Unless you make yourself useful; why don't you put a spell on the mill so it grinds the corn and makes the flour all by itself? Save us a job.

PERI: Well it might, but that's not what I'm here for. I made a promise to your dad when he put a turbocharger on my broomstick; not only am I the fairest and finest witch around but these days I'm also the fastest. Makes a real difference when you're in need of a quick getaway – just a pity he didn't get round to building a warp drive. No – I made a promise to keep an eye on you four; he knew if I didn't that you'd let everything he'd built up go to rack and ruin.

WAYNE: That's hardly fair!

SHANE: As if we would!

PERI: You two would. But today I'm here to stop Michael make a mess of things.

MICHAEL: Me? What have I done?

PERI: Nothing – yet; that's the problem. I couldn't help overhearing you Michael – I think you should be very grateful that your dad left you the cat.

MICHAEL: Why on earth should I be?

PERI: Because – he'll be the making of you.

WAYNE: You have to be joking!

SHANE: All he's good for is sleeping and eating.

JANE: I could say the same for you.

PERI: I never joke about my craft. Trust me, I'm a witch. *(She goes over to the basket and recites.)*

> This cat will be your fortune
>
> If given half a chance.
>
> Therefore our first challenge
>
> Is to wake him from his trance.
>
> So Tom, it's time you wakened
>
> And stood up on your paws.
>
> Become an action feline
>
> Teeth and fur and claws!

(There is a flash and blackout. Everyone jumps back; TOM stretches and dusts himself down.)

TOM: Talk about a rude awakening! I was fast asleep, having a lovely dream about mice with clogs on so I could hear 'em coming. *(All, except PERI who looks pleased with herself, stare at TOM open mouthed.)*

JANE: Blimey! He can talk!

TOM: Course I can! With my breeding, did you expect anything less?

WAYNE: You've never spoken to us before.

TOM: That's because you've never had anything interesting to say.

MICHAEL: Thanks a bunch, Peri! You've managed to turn that cat into a catastrophe! How am I supposed to feed him – he'll have an appetite like a tiger!

PERI: Never fear, you'll find a way.

SHANE: And I know what that way is; you can earn your keep by sorting out any rats left in the mill. I just hope they're not as big as you.

TOM: I've had enough of catching rats to last my nine lives. It's time I branched out – I'll become a cat burglar.

JANE: What's the point of burgling cats? They don't own anything worth stealing – except perhaps their fur coats.

WAYNE: It's very simple; if you want to stay here you work. No work – no food.

SHANE: He'd make a nice rug though. Brighten up the parlour no end. *(TOM looks horrified.)*

MICHAEL: I'm beginning to agree, you great layabout. Huh! That makes three of you now.

PERI: Wrong. I wouldn't have bothered transforming Tom, if I didn't have a purpose in mind.

TOM: Yes, listen to her, please. Forget the rats; I've got an idea that might just make Michael's fortune. *(To MICHAEL.)* I belong to you now, so your success is my success – we sink or swim together. Trust me – we'll be rich.

WAYNE: Have you been on the catnip again?

SHANE: Believe that, you'll believe anything.

JANE: If he was all black at least he might be lucky. That would be something.

TOM: Now, now! You're all doubting Thomas – you haven't seen what I can do when I put my mind to it. So Michael follow me and – trust me.

MICHAEL: Do I have any choice? But this had better work whatever it is, or I'll catapult you over the mill.

JANE: I'll come with you; I want to see what he's up to.

WAYNE: Leave us out of it.

SHANE: No good'll come of colluding with a cat! *(They exit.)*

PERI: I must go too – I have other work to do. Go with Tom and do what he says Michael; but whatever he tells you, keep it quiet – don't let the cat out of the bag! *(She exits.)*

JANE: Lead the way then Tom; I don't know what you've got planned, but if you make our fortune I'll say you're the cats whiskers!

MICHAEL: I second that! *(They exit; curtain.)*

Scene Four

Out in the country. On the lower stage or in front of half tabs. The rabbits enter and begin grazing happily in the sunshine.

1ST RABBIT: What a beautiful day!

2ND RABBIT: *(Looking warily about.)* Nothing to spoil the peace, no danger on the horizon.

1ST RABBIT: Just the sort of day for us rabbits to indulge in a good old hop about.

Song and dance routine: possibly 'At the hop', DANNY and the Juniors. As the dance ends, TOM, MICHAEL and JANE enter; TOM is carrying a very large sack. They form a huddle and speak in stage whispers to begin with.

TOM: This'll do – just the place; now – remember what I told you.

JANE: I'm not sure about this – I like bunny rabbits.

MICHAEL: Don't be such a softy; do as Tom says.

TOM: *(Turning to the rabbits.)* Hello rabbits; nice day isn't it?

1ST RABBIT: Maybe it is, but that doesn't explain what you humans are doing here, invading our territory.

MICHAEL: Just looking for inspiration.

2ND RABBIT: There's no one here with a name like that.

JANE: It ain't a person, silly – it's a thing.

1ST RABBIT: What is it then?

TOM: Somewhere between perspiration and desperation.

2ND RABBIT: Oh, very clever! Anyway, what do you want – you're trespassing.

JANE: Er, um – that is, we……

TOM: Never you mind; it's a secret. *(TOM, MICHAEL and JANE peer intently into the sack; TOM shakes it – there is the sound as of coins chinking.)*

1ST RABBIT: *(Very curious.)* What's in that bag?

TOM: Oh nothing important – don't let it bother you. *(TOM, MICHAEL and JANE all try to look innocent.)*

2ND RABBIT: It must be something special, otherwise you lot wouldn't be staring at it.

MICHAEL: Well if you must know….. *(Whispering.)* it's treasure!

TOM/JANE: Sssh!

1ST RABBIT: I don't believe you.

TOM: Suit yourself. *(TOM, MICHAEL and JANE peer into the sack again, making explanations of delight.)*

2ND RABBIT: *(Overcome with curiosity.)* Let's have a look then!

JANE: No; we couldn't possibly let you see.

1ST RABBIT: I knew there was nothing in there – you're just showing off!

JANE: No, we're not!

RABBITS: Yes you are!

TOM: Oh, very well; come and have a look if you must. We'll get no peace 'till you do. *(The second rabbit peers into the sack.)*

2ND RABBIT: There's nothing in here! *(Still with his head in the sack.)*

TOM: There is now! In with him! *(TOM, MICHAEL and JANE grab the RABBIT and push it kicking into the sack. All the other rabbits scream and scatter offstage.)* There you are – worked like a charm; these rabbits are so gullible. *(Examining his claws. The RABBIT wriggles in the sack.)*

JANE: Poor ickle bunny. Now, you promise not to hurt him?

TOM: That's up to the King; depends how hungry he is. Now I have to go to the palace; but first you need to find me a hat and some boots.

MICHAEL: What on earth for? You're a cat – cats don't wear hats!

TOM: This one does. Anyway, I have to make a good impression if I'm to represent the Marquis of Carabas to the King.

JANE: Marquis? What Marquis? We don't know anyone posh like that.

TOM: Yes we do – Michael. So, come on; boots and a hat first and then off to the palace. *(They exit. As they go the OGRE and his IMPS enter through the curtain.)*

OGRE: Now I wonder what they're up to? We'll find out soon enough – nothing escapes my gaze. But look! We have an audience. *(He addresses the audience directly.)* They say you get what you deserve; well, you deserve me. As they haven't let me have an appearance for ages, you've probably got all relaxed and comfortable – I'll soon put a stop to that! I'm very put out. As the most attractive and important character, I should have the most to say. But what do they give me? A few measly lines that's what! Someone will pay for such a slight. After all there's no point in being the villain of the piece unless there are plenty of opportunities to frighten the children and make their parents lives a misery. But I don't have the time to deal properly with you just now as I have work for my spies. *(He turns to the imps, selecting two of them.)* You and you! Go across the river, get into the palace somehow and find out what's going on. You know what you have to do?

2 IMPS: Of course, master!

OGRE: Then what are you waiting for? On your way! *(He shoos the two imps ahead of him and exits with the others.)*

Scene Five

The palace. On stage are the KING, QUEEN, PRINCESS, BIB and TUCKER and courtiers.

QUEEN: *(To the KING.)* It's no good; she'll have to go.

KING: Who, dear?

QUEEN: You haven't been listening! Your daughter, of course!

KING: Why, what's she done?

PRINCESS: Nothing, father; mother just wants to see me married off and out of your hair.

KING: I'm sure that's not true!

QUEEN: Yes it is. Eating us out of house and home and taking up space. Spending all her time in her room listening to that awful *(Latest group)*. Pretending she's a finalist on madrigal idol.

PRINCESS: If there was someone I wanted to spend my life with, I'd go like a shot. But there's no one around here that I could possibly love.

QUEEN: What's love got to do with it, pray?

Song: possibly 'What's Love Got To Do With It', Tina Turner.

QUEEN: Marry for love? In my day you would have had no choice.

BIB: In her day you got carried off by a caveman.

QUEEN: What did you say?

TUCKER: He said all would have been your slave, ma'am.

QUEEN: How kind and how true.

KING: But my dear, we can't force our daughter to marry someone she doesn't love. It would be a recipe for disaster. *(Aside.)* Rather like your cooking.

QUEEN: I admit it's not ideal; but we're running out of time. She'll be left on the shelf.

TUCKER: *(Aside.)* Better to be left on the shelf than be as plain as a wardrobe.

QUEEN: I didn't catch that. *(She sneezes loudly and searches in vain for a handkerchief. Failing to find one she uses the KING's sleeve.)* Although there isn't much I don't catch.

BIB: He said beware of microbes. Oh, and that he quite agrees – something must be done. *(There is the sound of a doorbell, far away in the deepest recesses of the palace.)*

KING: Oh, bother! Someone see who that is at the door. If it's another lamprey salesman, tell him that we already have a surfeit of them. *(The bell rings again.)*

QUEEN: Well don't just stand there Bib! Go and answer the door.

BIB: Why me? It's always me – it's not fair. You all seem to forget that Tucker and I are stylists. When we say we're dressers it means we look after the King's clothes – we're not part of the fixtures and fittings. Anyway, those doors are so heavy that last time I opened them I nearly broke my wrist.

QUEEN: The job of doorman would suit you – it's tailor made! All part of life's rich pattern. But I warn you, if you don't go this instant, we'll be fitting you for a concrete overcoat!

KING: Now, now dear! Don't get hot under the collar! No need for such a dressing down.

TUCKER: *(To BIB.)* You'd better shift; get moving before she makes any alterations! *(Aside.)* She's really needled. *(BIB exits hastily; there is the sound of running feet, then of a door creaking slowly open.)*

KING: I must put some WD40 on those hinges. *(More running feet; BIB appears.)*

BIB: If it please your Majesties, there's a cat at the door craving an audience. He has a sack with him, which seems to be moving.

QUEEN: A cat! Don't let it anywhere near me – it's probably got fleas. And it'll make my nose run, there'll be fur everywhere. Nasty, dirty creatures!

BIB: Actually, your Majesty, this cat is very smart – for a cat. Quite a fashionable feline.

KING: No, the Queen's right, we can't have her sneezing all night. Send it away.

BIB: It's Tucker's turn this time. That cat's put me all in a tizz.

TUCKER: Oh, alright, I'll go. Don't go on! *(He exits; there is the sound of running feet, the creaking door and feet returning.)* He won't take no for an answer. He says a cat may look at a King.

PRINCESS: One moment! Did you say 'he says'?

TUCKER: Didn't I mention it? As well as being smart, he talks. Mind you, he's got a rotten taste in hats. Like an advert for What Not To Wear.

PRINCESS: Never mind that. A cat that talks! This I must see; invite him in father.

KING: I think that I shall – the Queen will just have to sneeze. Go and fetch him.

TUCKER: No need Sire; I anticipated your orders, he's already here.

TOM enters, dragging his sack. He bows to the KING, the QUEEN and PRINCESS, doffing his hat.

TOM: Your Majesties.

QUEEN: Keep away from me!

TOM: Don't worry your Majesty I had a wash this morning; well more like a lick and a promise.

BIB: Well, get him. Who's a smarty paws then?

TUCKER: Fancy that – a puss in boots. What on earth does a cat need with a pair of boots? Paws not good enough?

TOM: I'll have you know boots are essential for a cat who wants to go places. Listen.

Song: possibly 'These boots are made for walking'.

PRINCESS: Well cat – what is it you want?

BIB: Speak up, tell his Majesty.

TOM: Sire, I have a present from my master, the Marquis of Carabas.

QUEEN: Never heard of him. *(She sneezes.)*

TOM: His lands lie many leagues from here, across the river. He wishes to present his respects and with your permission to pay court to your daughter, the Princess.

QUEEN: Is he rich?

PRINCESS: Mother! Is money all you think of?

KING: She has a point, you know. You must be kept in the manner to which you have become accustomed. So cat – is he rich?

TOM: But of course, your Majesty. He possesses many jewels, paintings, sumptuous fabrics and tapestries. His lands are extensive and fertile, with forests, vineyards and orchards.

BIB: He sounds promising.

TUCKER: Any jobs going?

TOM: Knowing your Majesty's taste, he's sent this present as evidence of his good intentions. *(All this time the sack has been moving, creating a source of fascination for the courtiers.)* May I show you?

KING: It isn't dangerous, I hope?

TOM: No Sire, not dangerous at all. *(He opens the sack and tips out the RABBIT, who sits there shivering with fright.)* Knowing your Majesty's taste for game, here is the finest, fattest rabbit from my master's warrens. As you see, still very fresh.

QUEEN: A rabbit! More fur! It's all too much! *(She faints and is attended to by courtiers, who apply smelling salts from a very large bottle.)*

KING: Never mind her, happens all the time. Fur, feather or fin, it's all the same – she can't stand them. But I can – there's nothing I like more than rabbit pie! *(At this, the RABBIT collapses in a heap, utterly terrified.)*

BIB: Can we have the skin?

TUCKER: Fur accessories are in this year.

PRINCESS: No you can't! Father, how could you? Look at the poor little thing; I forbid you to put it in a pie. Give it to me and I'll keep it as a pet. *(She goes to comfort the RABBIT. Then to TOM.)* Thank your master for us.

TOM: This is but a foretaste, there'll be more evidence of his good faith in the coming days.

QUEEN: *(Reviving.)* Please, no more wildlife!

KING: *(Aside to TOM.)* Ignore her; you know my tastes it seems. The tastier the better. But when shall we meet this master of yours?

TOM: Soon, but only when he's convinced you of his good intentions. Now, I must take my leave. *(He bows and exits, followed by BIB and TUCKER.)*

PRINCESS: Well, I've never met an ambassador quite like that before; personally, I can't wait to meet this Marquis.

KING: Me too!

Act 1 PUSS IN BOOTS 25

Scene Six

The mill kitchen – represented by a simple trestles and worktop combination or similar. On lower stage or in front of half tabs. MICHAEL, JANE, WAYNE, SHANE and TOM enter. JANE is carrying a very large cookery book, which she places on the worktop and starts to leaf through it.

JANE: *(Reading.)* Take three pounds of best flour. *(She places a large brown paper bag of 'flour' into a bowl.)*

MICHAEL: No problems finding that then; if flour was gold dust we'd be rolling.

JANE: We will be once I've made the pastry.

MICHAEL: No, I mean money; oh, never mind – let's get on with it. What's that book you're using – I've never seen it before.

JANE: It's Delia's latest – "Lighter meals: how to manage on only fourteen courses". Next, take fifteen large, fresh eggs. Michael, go outside and frighten the chickens; but not too much or we'll have scrambled eggs.

WAYNE: What a waste! My best flour and my breakfast all used up.

SHANE: And what's all this in aid of? It's not my birthday for months.

JANE: It's not for you. It's for Michael.

WAYNE: It's not his birthday either. Even if it was, we shouldn't waste a good cake on him.

TOM: It's not for Michael exactly; no, it's part of my master plan to soften up the King and Queen and to help Michael create the right impression. When the cake is cooked, I'll be taking it to the palace.

WAYNE: Oh, I see. It has to make the right impression does it?

SHANE: In that case it'll need a few special ingredients.

WAYNE and SHANE seize various jars and boxes and proceed to tip their contents into the bowl. JANE and MICHAEL try in vain to stop them.

WAYNE: Cayenne pepper and chili powder!

SHANE: Soap flakes and drain cleaner!

WAYNE: Worcester sauce!

SHANE: Mustard!

WAYNE: Vinegar!

SHANE: The piece de resistance – curry powder!

WAYNE: More curry powder!

SHANE: Can't have too much curry powder!

> *All this while, JANE has been shouting 'Stop, stop! You'll ruin it' etc. As SHANE throws in more curry powder, there is a large bang. This could possibly be achieved with a large Party Popper; confetti is scattered in all directions preferably over the protagonists. Everyone dives for cover; there is a pause for the 'smoke' to clear, before they clamber to their feet. They all peer into the bowl at the ruins of the cake.*

MICHAEL: Is it safe to come out yet?

WAYNE: Wow! What a recipe!

SHANE: That's the best yet; what a result!

TOM: Personally, I'd have included some powdered mouse – seems to give it body. And maybe a beak or two and some feet to give it that delightful crunch.

JANE: Now look what you've done! Just as I said you would, you've gone and ruined it. You, you, culinary criminals you! We'll have start all over again.

MICHAEL: I don't know why we bother anyway. All these presents may impress the King and Queen, but as soon as they see me in the flesh –

WAYNE: What a horrible thought!

MICHAEL: All this effort will have gone to waste. I've got no posh clothes – nothing remotely suitable to wear to court. I've got no real title – only the one this loony cat has dreamt up. And no two coins to rub together, let alone untold riches and lands. It'll take them about two seconds to rumble me and then I'll have as much chance to win the Princess as fly to the moon!

WAYNE: He's got a point you know.

SHANE: Seems to sum up the situation nicely.

TOM: I must admit, it could be a problem; there are some things I can't provide. *(He scratches his head; PERI enters, unseen at first. She coughs. They all jump when they see her.)*

JANE: I wish you wouldn't do that! Creeping up on people when they're not expecting it – it's not nice. Nearly gave me a heart attack!

PERI: Terribly sorry! But I was just on the flightpath passing overhead when I heard Michael complaining about his lot.

The following dialogue is quick fire.

JANE: His what?

WAYNE: A plot?

SHANE: A spot?

TOM: His yacht?

MICHAEL: You're hot.

PERI: His lot! His state of being; his condition; his station in life; his modal existence. *(They all stare at her, open-mouthed.)* Basically, he feels he's going nowhere.

Song: possibly "Nowhere man", The Beatles, started by PERI, joined by JANE, WAYNE and SHANE. Ideally, JANE will have a solo during the song.

JANE: Oh, I see. Why didn't you say so the first time?

MICHAEL: Well, what's the answer? How am I ever going to pass myself off as a rich lord?

WAYNE: Shouldn't be a problem. Do what you always do.

SHANE: You've been passing yourself off as something special for years.

PERI: Don't despair Michael. All we have to do is to create the right situation and Tom is the very cat to do it. You can all start clearing up this mess, while I have a quiet word with Tom. *(She leads TOM towards the audience and bends to speak to him, while the others clear away the 'kitchen' and exit.)*

Tom, in order to make an impression,
We're going to create a disaster.
To add to his sense of depression,
We'll drown young Michael, your master! *(TOM looks as appalled as a cat can.)*

TOM: You can't be serious!

PERI: Don't look so worried, my whiskery friend,
We'll only pretend that he's drowning.
Trust me – he'll be fine in the end.
You'll spoil your looks with that frowning! *(She leads TOM offstage, all the time whispering in his ear.)*

Act 1 — PUSS IN BOOTS

Scene Seven

The palace. On stage are the KING and QUEEN, the PRINCESS, BIB and TUCKER and the courtiers. During the early part of the action the two imps emerge from the wings and sit quietly at one side of the stage; they watch the proceedings intently.

PRINCESS: Will you please stop going on about marriage! It's really getting on my nerves.

QUEEN: All you have to do is to make a decision; there are plenty of potential suitors, but you miss 'pick and choosy' have rejected the lot.

PRINCESS: That's because none of them measure up, rather like the clothes these two make. *(Indicating BIB and TUCKER.)*

BIB: For a princess you can be really cutting at times.

TUCKER: Well, she's got you sewn up.

BIB: And given you a dressing down.

TUCKER: There's a pattern emerging here.

BIB: Well – if the cap fits.

KING: Careful you two! Your jobs are hanging by a thread. But maybe this Marquis of Carabas we hear so much about is the one. You must admit that he's very generous.

QUEEN: It's alright for you; every present he's sent so far has either made me sneeze or brought me out in a rash.

PRINCESS: He may well be generous, but that's probably to make up for the fact that he's short, fat, ugly, bald, has bad breath and wears flared tights and sandals.

KING: But my dear, nobody's perfect.

QUEEN: Absolutely; look at you.

PRINCESS: How many times do I have to tell you? I won't marry anyone I don't love. The attraction has to be there.

QUEEN: Stuff and nonsense! What counts is family duty, continuing our illustrious line and most of all adding to our wealth and lands.

PRINCESS: Mother, you're so horribly mercenary! And I don't want to end up like you two – always bickering.

QUEEN: Bickering? Us? We never bicker, do we dear?

KING: Only when I don't agree with you.

QUEEN: Exactly. And you know better than to disagree with me.

KING: But dear, sometimes I do know better than you; there are things that I can do and you can't.

QUEEN: Nonsense, I can do anything better than you!

Song: possibly a short section of 'I can do anything better than you'. As the song ends there is the sound of the doorbell.

BIB: Alright, don't say it; I'm going. No doubt I'll adjust to the role of doorman.

TUCKER: As the Queen said, tailor made for you. I bet that it's that cat again. *(BIB exits. Once more there is the sound of running feet, the door opening and running feet returning. BIB re-enters.)*

BIB: *(Out of breath.)* Your M-M-Majesties, may I p-p-present Tom cat the servant to the Marquis of Carabas.

TUCKER: See, I was right again – on the button. *(TOM enters carrying a large and perfect cake, which he hands to a courtier. He bows and sweeps off his hat.)*

TOM: Your Majesties, I bring you another gift from my master, the Marquis.

QUEEN: Don't come any closer, I don't want your fur balls anywhere near me.

TOM: Perish the thought, majesty. I bring you this beautiful cake.

QUEEN: I can see that; what sort of cake?

TOM: A fruit cake your majesty – it somehow seems to suit the court. Plenty more fruit cakes here I see. It's a cake made with the choicest fruits, nuts, seeds and some special ingredients of my own catch – I mean making.

QUEEN: It sounds horrible; no doubt I shall be allergic to it.

Act 1   PUSS IN BOOTS   31

KING: Ta very much – much appreciated. We'll put it with all your other presents; the nine partridges, the eight collared doves, the seven grouse, the six fresh salmon, the five cock pheasants, the four fallow deer, the three wild boar, the two white geese and the one rabbit – I can't help thinking that you skimped on the rabbit.

If time and resources allow, this could be an opportunity for a song and /or dance. Children could enter dressed as the above animals, or could carry on 'cut outs' to represent them which would be a simpler solution. They would leave the stage at the end of the song.

BIB: Amazing how much road kill there is about these days. I blame the increase in heavy carts.

TUCKER: One doesn't know whether to start a zoo or a taxidermy business.

BIB: Mind you; all that fur and feather will come in handy for next year's collections.

TUCKER: I can just feel a fur and feather year coming on.

QUEEN: And every one of them makes me sneeze or break out in lumps, so think again when it comes to dressing me. *(To TOM.)* Why can't you bring us any inanimate presents, like money or jewels?

KING: Hush dear; I'm sure that we are all very grateful to the Marquis.

PRINCESS: Tom, all these presents are very impressive, but when shall we meet this oh-so-generous Marquis? Is he afraid to show his face? Is it that bad?

TOM: Not in the least, Princess. In fact that's why I'm here – to propose a meeting. *(The two IMPS crane forward to better hear what is being said. They stay focussed for the rest of the scene.)* I understand that it's your family custom to walk by the river on fine days. The seaweed on my wall tells me that tomorrow will be fine. My master plans to meet you by the river – his lands lie across it.

PRINCESS: But I thought that those lands belong to the Ogre. No one ever goes there – not even father's troops; everyone is too terrified. Are they no longer owned by the Ogre?

TOM: *(After some hesitation.)* Yes and no.

KING: What do you mean? Yes and no?

TOM: Yes, they belong to the Ogre. And no, not for much longer. *(The IMPS look at each other meaningfully.)*

QUEEN: I knew that it was too good to be true. It's all too far-fetched.

TOM: My master has made him an offer he can't refuse.

KING: I'd have liked to be there when he did.

TOM: Come to the riverbank tomorrow and you'll see that it's true. It's the only favour that my master asks.

PRINCESS: That's sounds fair. I'll come even if no one else will. I want to know what lies behind all this mystery.

KING: And we'll come too, won't we dear?

QUEEN: Very well. If you insist.

KING: For once I do. There's nothing I like more than the opportunity to play Pooh Sticks and to watch the river flow.

Act One finale song: possibly 'Watching The River Flow', Bob Dylan. The IMPS slip away unnoticed from the stage, as the curtains close.

ACT TWO

Scene One

A short overture; as the music dies away once again there is dim green lighting, wisps of smoke, lightning and distant thunder. As before, the imps precede the OGRE onto the lower stage or in front of half tabs. One of the IMPS carries the 'Seeing Bowl'; the OGRE stirs the water and peers into it.

OGRE: I know that they're up to something, but what? There are clouds in the water and I can't for the life of me make out what's happening. The line speed here is rubbish – the picture keeps buffering! I'll just have to pay for fibre – trust me to find a castle in an area with no coverage. Bother! Bother! Bother! This is making me angry! *(The IMPS exchange worried glances.)*

1ST IMP: There's no need to get angry, your magnificence.

2ND IMP: We have news for you.

OGRE: Come here then and tell me your news. It had better be good! *(He bends to listen as the two imps whisper in his ears. We hear scraps of their conversation:* 'Marquis'...... 'Princess'...... 'meeting by the river'...... 'your lands'...... 'offer you can't refuse'...... 'tomorrow'. *The OGRE straightens up to his full height.)* So, that's their little game is it? Pathetic! Some foolish upstart of a human thinks he can take possession of my lands, does he? I'll teach him to underestimate my power! And that fool of a king has believed this nonsense; well, well, we'll see about that. He'll pay dearly for his credulity. *(A pause.)* I think it's high time we paid a visit to the palace – perhaps when they're in the middle of one of their little soirees. What a bourgeois lot they are – well here comes the revolution! I'll lead them in a merry dance which they won't forget in a hurry. Think they can take my lands do they? I'll take their land and make the king and his entire court my slaves, assuming I don't grind their miserable bones to dust first. And while I'm at it, I'll carry off their precious Princess to be my bride. They won't be so proud then. *(Turning to his imps.)* And you'll help me do it; any slacking and you know what to expect! And here's where their heartaches begin!

Song: possibly 'Heartache Tonight', The Eagles. The imps follow him as he sweeps off stage.

Act 2   PUSS IN BOOTS

Scene Two

Outside the mill. MICHAEL, JANE, WAYNE, SHANE, PERI and TOM are on stage.

TOM: Now listen carefully, Michael, here's my plan.

PERI: Who's plan, Tom?

TOM: Oh, alright; your plan. Credit where it's due I suppose. *(He becomes expansive.)* Imagine the scene. The King and the whole court, including the Princess of course, are in stately procession, on their way to meet you at the river. When you see them nearby, you go for a swim.

JANE: That don't seem right. He'll end up all wet.

WAYNE: No change there then.

MICHAEL: Do you think that me in my old bathing cozzie is going to impress the princess?

SHANE: Not when she sees bits of you through the holes in it, it won't.

MICHAEL: When I come out they're going to see that my other clothes are old and patched as well.

PERI: There's more to it than that. You're still in the river; when the King and the court are near enough, you start waving like mad.

JANE: That's a bit familiar; you won't have been introduced.

TOM: You're not waving, you're drowning! Haven't you got it yet? You pretend you're drowning.

JANE: Not waving, but drowning? Where've I heard that before?

MICHAEL: I think some poet wrote it.

WAYNE: It's on the toilet wall then?

SHANE: Not the one that we use – I'd have seen it.

MICHAEL: That's hardly the point. Why do I have to pretend that I'm drowning when I can swim perfectly well?

WAYNE: Go on with you!

SHANE: No wonder you always look so clean.

MICHAEL: I tell you I can. Listen!

Song: possibly 'The Swimming Song', Loudon Wainwright Third.

MICHAEL: See, I told you!

PERI: We know that now, but the courtiers don't.

TOM: Then I start shouting for help. They're bound to respond.

MICHAEL: What if they don't? They won't want to get their posh togs wet.

SHANE: Then either you look a complete wazzock – or you drown.

TOM: Relax! The King will send people to rescue you – he's soft that way. When they drag you out, you must act helpless.

WAYNE: He'll be very convincing.

SHANE: He's had enough practice.

TOM: Everyone will be worried about you – especially the Princess.

MICHAEL: You think so?

TOM: Sure to be – it's a princess's job to be concerned for the underdog and you really fit the bill. We'll say that robbers have stolen your clothes; they're sure to lend you some – if only to preserve your modesty. Modesty!

WAYNE: I wonder which charity shop the King uses these days?

JANE: Don't be horrible. Michael will look very handsome in court clothes; everyone will think that he's one of them.

SHANE: We've known he's been one of them for years.

MICHAEL: It'll never work.

TOM: Trust me. You do your part and I'll do mine.

PERI: Between you, you'll convince them that you're the real thing – a genuine marquis. Just what we need! *(She spies a group of farm workers as they enter from the rear of the auditorium on the way to their fields. PERI stops them.)* Good day to you all; who is your foreman?

FOREMAN: I am. Who wants to know?

PERI: Never you mind. Listen, the King will pass through the fields by the river tomorrow. When he asks, you must tell him that they belong to the Marquis of Carabas.

FOREMAN: Never heard of him.

TOM: You have now and please do as she says.

FOREMAN: A talking cat! I've seen everything now. That's crazy. Cats can't talk.

PERI: True under normal circumstances – but I'm a witch. If you disobey me I'll turn you all into animals like I did with him.

TOM: Before she came along, I was a handsome prince. *(The workers all laugh.)*

FOREMAN: You'll have to do better than that, if you want to put the wind up us, won't she lads?

WORKERS: Yes!

PERI: I mean it.

WORKERS: Oh no, you don't!

OTHERS: Oh yes, she does!

PERI: In that case, it's drastic measures. If you don't do what I say, I'll make you sit through a year's worth of the omnibus editions of The Archers. You want to know all about modern farming, don't you? You won't be so cheerful then!

WORKERS: Anything but that! We'll do it!

PERI: Good! Thank you. Off you go; and don't forget, if the King asks, these lands belong to the Marquis of Carabas. *(The workers exit, perhaps singing a work song, which dies away in the distance.)*

JANE: You wouldn't really have made them suffer like that would you?

PERI: No, of course not. But that's for me to know and them to find out. Now, to work. *(All exit. The lights dim; sounds of thunder. The OGRE appears at the side of the stage, in a spotlight and flanked by his IMPS.)*

OGRE: So, they really plan to go through with it. I'll let them have their little moment of triumph at the river. One small detail they seem to have forgotten – how they're going to deal with me. Made me an offer I can't refuse. Pah! I'll let them think their plan is working; it'll be all the more fun when I turn the tables on them and confront them at the palace. And with a bit of luck that boy will forget how to swim and drown. *(He pauses.)* But even if he does, it changes nothing. Roll on tomorrow and <u>my</u> moment of triumph! Come, imps! *(He exits, perhaps singing a reprise of 'Heartaches Tonight', which dies away as his imps follow him.)*

Act 2 — PUSS IN BOOTS

Scene Three

In the country, by the river. On the lower stage or in front of half tabs. THE KING, QUEEN, PRINCESS, BIB, TUCKER and the courtiers enter.

QUEEN: Where is he then, this Marquis? I knew he wouldn't be here; obviously unreliable and not to be trusted. Just too good to be true – what did I tell you? And what's that funny smell?

KING: It's fresh air, dear.

QUEEN: I don't like it. Can't you do something? It's bad for my sinuses.

KING: I'll have it changed. But you must be patient and give the Marquis time; it's not done to be early.

QUEEN: Not done? I'll give him not done; I'll have him done to a turn.

PRINCESS: *(Looking offstage.)* Look! There's someone waving. *(There is a distant muffled shout, which could be "help, help".)*

QUEEN: Ignore them; it's probably just one of my fans. But waving – how common! *(Again there comes the shout of "help", but this time somewhat clearer.)*

KING: It almost sounds like someone shouting for help.

PRINCESS: That's exactly what it is; shouldn't someone go and see what's wrong? *(At that moment, TOM runs on, dishevelled and gasping for breath.)*

TOM: H-h-h-help! My master, the Marquis is drowning!

QUEEN: Is that who was waving?

TOM: Yes, but only to attract attention.

QUEEN: It's not done to draw attention to oneself – it's undignified.

TOM: So is drowning! Now, if you please, can somebody help to rescue him?

KING: I suppose somebody better had; who can we send?

PRINCESS: Send these two old soaks! *(Pointing to BIB and TUCKER.)* It won't matter if they get wet. They're wet enough already. You two, to the riverbank and the rescue. Now!

BIB: But we'll get all muddy, and I've already had a wash this week.

TUCKER: And just think who and what has been in that river before us!

KING: Enough! Go and haul him out and I might let you off the hook. Now, before he becomes fish food! If you're successful you'll be our best Bib and Tucker.

BIB: Well, if you're going to take that line.....

TUCKER: There has to be a catch; the net result is sure to be that we hit bottom.

TOM: *(Aside.)* At last they've taken the bait. *(To all.)* Will you please get on with it? There's a limit to how long he can tread water.

QUEEN: What did you say?

TOM: I said, please listen to your daughter.

KING: Yes, get on with it you two!

BIB: Very well. If you insist!

TUCKER: Alright! Don't nag. We're going. *(They run offstage. All turn to watch their progress; there are shouts from the courtiers such as "They've got him", "No, they've missed", "They'll fall in", "Try again", "Almost there", "They've landed him", "He's safe" etc. There is a burst of applause.)*

KING: They're carrying him back.

PRINCESS: He looks done for.

> *BIB and TUCKER stagger on, dragging MICHAEL between them. Ideally they should be stripped down to colourful underwear, covered in water weed and somewhat wet. MICHAEL is resplendent in an old fashioned striped bathing costume.*

BIB: Just look at me; I've had another bath and it's not even my birthday.

TUCKER: And that water hasn't been warmed at all; I'm freezing and I'm bound to catch a cold.

QUEEN: If you come near me with your nasty germs, you'll catch a lot more than a cold.

PRINCESS: You're all wasting time; put him down and let's see if we can revive him! *(BIB and TUCKER lay MICHAEL down and step away.)*

KING: I think he's dead.

PRINCESS: No he isn't.

KING: I think he <u>is</u>.

PRINCESS: No he isn't – he just needs mouth-to-mouth resuscitation.

QUEEN: Leave it to me, I know just what to do. *(She begins to bend over MICHAEL; as she does he opens his eyes and sits bolt upright.)*

MICHAEL: I'm fine! Really, I'm fine!

KING: What an amazing recovery.

QUEEN: And I didn't even have to touch him. Pity – that's one contamination I wouldn't have minded.

MICHAEL: *(Remembering the situation.)* Where am I? What happened?

PRINCESS: *(Kneeling by him.)* You're safe now; you nearly drowned.

MICHAEL: You must be the Princess – thank you for your concern; it makes a soaking worthwhile. But forgive my appearance – I didn't intend to greet you in this state. Tom! Where are my clothes?

TOM: I'm sorry, master. They've disappeared; someone must have stolen them when I ran for help. They must have been tempted by all the rich velvet and gold brocade. So much so that they left you to drown.

BIB: Velvet and brocade sounds nice.

TUCKER: But rather last season, don't you think?

BIB: Yes, and anyway I don't like the cut of his cloth!

KING: Stealing your clothes? That's too bad! One can't trust anyone these days, can one? But let me help; I've lots of clothes I don't wear anymore – something is bound to fit you. Bib! Tucker! Take the Marquis to the palace and fit him out with some clothes from my wardrobe. But whatever you do, don't give away my old blue suede shoes – I'm very attached to them.

Song: possibly 'Blue suede shoes', Elvis Presley, sung by the KING with help from BIB and TUCKER. The KING is completely out of his normal character for this.

BIB: This is a turn up; us as heroes of the hour.

TUCKER: But don't make a habit of drowning yourself, young man.....

BIB: It's not the fashion.

TUCKER: You're not cut out for a swimmer.

BIB: You don't have a flair for it.

TUCKER: Leave it to us your Majesty, we'll dive deep into the recesses of your wardrobe.

BIB: And when it comes to fashion, he'll soon be in the swim.

KING: Do be quiet, you're giving me a headache! Take the Marquis and get him dressed! *(BIB and TUCKER bow to the KING and lead MICHAEL offstage.)* Now, let's get the lie of the land. *(He shades his eyes and peers in all directions.)* These fields go on as far as the eye can see.

QUEEN: But are they all his as he says? I don't believe it for a moment, and even if they are his I'm sure they are all genetically modified.

PRINCESS: Don't be ridiculous Mother! Anyway, we can soon find out who owns these fields. Let's ask them. *(The farm workers enter led by the FOREMAN, perhaps singing the work song, which dies away as they approach the royal party.)*

QUEEN: I say, peasant!

PRINCESS: Mother, you can't speak to them like that! It's not PC. *(Turning to the FOREMAN.)* Please answer a question for us as we can't agree. Whose fields are these which lie all around us? *(The workers all look at each other.)*

FOREMAN: *(Sweeping off his hat and bowing.)* Why Princess, they all belong to the Marquis of.... *(He pauses and scratches his head.)*

WORKERS: Carabas!

FOREMAN: The Marquis of Carabas, of course.

QUEEN: All of them? *(The workers again look at each other.)*

FOREMAN: All of them, your majesty.

KING: You don't seem very sure.

FOREMAN: It is only that we're nervous, your majesty. We're not used to such august company.

QUEEN: Fair enough; I can quite understand why you might be nervous when someone as important as me deigns to speak to you. I must say that having all this land is certainly a point in the Marquis's favour.

KING: Now that all that's settled, let's make our way back to the palace and see how they're getting on.

All exit, led by the KING, QUEEN and PRINCESS. As soon as they are offstage JANE and the RABBITS come through the curtains.

JANE: *(To the audience.)* I don't know about you, but I'm all of a dither. Has everything gone to plan? I'm a bag of nerves; I need something to calm me down. Now what could it be? Of course! You've guessed! A nice song will do the trick and you and the rabbits can all join in. *(Song for audience participation, with JANE working the audience in the usual way.)* Well that was lovely. Thank you for your help, I feel a lot better now. I'm off to find the latest news from the riverbank. *(JANE and the RABBITS exit.)*

Scene Four

The palace; folding screens and a mirror suggest a dressing room. MICHAEL and TOM enter, followed by BIB and TUCKER. MICHAEL is already dressed in shirt and breeches; BIB approaches him with a jacket, while TUCKER carries a pair of shoes.

BIB: Here, try this for size.

TUCKER: No, shoes first. *(BIB tries to coax MICHAEL into the jacket, while TUCKER tries to fit MICHAEL's feet into the shoes.)*

MICHAEL: Steady on! Who do you think I am? Cinderella?

BIB: You're certainly no prince Charming.

TUCKER: More like an ugly sister!

TOM: Have you forgotten that you're addressing the Marquis of Carabas?

BIB: We only have his word for that; we're in deep waters with this one. I feel we've been hung out to dry.

TUCKER: The whole thing still seems fishy to me; we're all at sea. I'm still wondering what's the catch.

MICHAEL: Can we stop the watery references, please? I'm very grateful for your help today and for the clothes, but now will you let me finish dressing?

BIB: Please yourself.

TUCKER: I'm not happy.

TOM: What is it this time? Your backache, your stomach, fallen arches, trapped w.....

TUCKER: Not me! I'm not happy with him! *(Indicating MICHAEL.)*

TOM: Join the club.

MICHAEL: When you've all quite finished!

BIB: He means that he's unhappy with the finished product.

MICHAEL: Product? I'm not a product!

TUCKER: Bear with us dear boy. We take pride in our work.

BIB: Something's missing; you can't go until everything's perfect.

TOM: We could be here some time.

BIB: I know! He needs a wig; that's it – a wig!

TUCKER: You're right – he needs a syrup; a crowning glory. Let's try a few on him.

They delve into a box containing a selection of wigs – all shapes, all sizes and all totally unsuitable. They try them on the long-suffering MICHAEL, one after the other in rapid succession.

MICHAEL: Stop! Stop! That's enough – I feel like a sink mop; I'll do without, thanks.

TOM: I thought it was an improvement – we couldn't see your face.

BIB: On reflection I think he's right.

TUCKER: He did look a bit hair raising. *(The KING, QUEEN and PRINCESS enter.)*

KING: *(Looking at MICHAEL.)* That's better; rather more decorous; take my advice young man, don't go swimming again – stick to terra firma.

QUEEN: Water washes off the insulation.

PRINCESS: I have to say he does look a whole lot better, that swimsuit wasn't exactly flattering. That's done the trick for the master, *(Turning to TOM.)* but I do think that such a fine ambassador should be equally smart; the fur coat is fine for outdoors but not for formal wear. I think Tom should wear a proper coat and a smart new hat, to keep up appearances.

MICHAEL: Yes, good idea!

TOM: Me? Wear a coat? Much too hot and restricting. Shan't!

ALL: Oh yes, you will!

TOM: Oh no, I won't! *(MICHAEL, BIB and TUCKER seize TOM and force him into a smart frock coat, jamming a new, garish, plumed hat on his head. TOM still struggles, so they don't let go.)* You'll have to let go some time. I shan't keep them on.

ALL: Oh yes, you will!

TOM: Oh no, I won't!

PRINCESS: I think you will; take a look at yourself. *(She holds up the mirror; as soon as TOM catches sight of himself he relaxes, strokes his whiskers and generally preens.)*

TOM: Maybe I will keep them on – but only under sufferance. *(He catches sight of himself in the mirror again and strikes a pose.)* Purrfect! Those feminine felines don't stand a chance.

MICHAEL: Tom, you're so vain!

Song: possibly 'You're so vain', Carly Simon or 'Dedicated follower of fashion', The Kinks, sung by all except TOM who struts about in his new finery.

KING: My stomach tells me that it'll soon be time for dinner; Marquis, you and your furry ambassador are invited of course, but I think that it's time we met the other members of your family. I presume you do have a family?

MICHAEL: Indeed I do; my father's dead, but I have a mother and two brothers.

PRINCESS: Then they're invited too; we'll send a messenger with the invitation.

MICHAEL: *(Panicking.)* No, no! I wouldn't dream of putting anyone to the trouble. Tom can go – he knows the way. He can put them in the picture.

TOM: *(Aside.)* Ever felt that you've been framed?

KING: No doubt you have an extensive family tree; a family as noble as yours must go back many generations. The flower of chivalry.

TOM: *(Aside.)* Yes graded Grains make finer flour.

MICHAEL: I have to say that we're more self made than noble.

TOM: *(Aside.)* More like self-raising. But at last they're going to go up in the world; looks like they're on a Grain elevator.

KING: Never mind, we all have to start somewhere. Now come along, there are lots of preparations to be made; we need to plan the menu for a start – I think moussaka and ratatouille for the cat!

PRINCESS: You go on, I'll follow in a moment. *(All exit, except the PRINCESS. The curtains close as she comes forward to the lower stage or in front of half tabs. The screens and mirror are struck.)* For the first time ever I feel that there's someone I could come to love. Let's hope that all his claims turn out to be true.

Song: possibly 'Closest thing to crazy' Katie Melua or 'Why does it always rain on me', Travis. As the song finishes the PRINCESS exits and the curtains open to reveal the Palace once more.

Scene Five

On stage are the KING, QUEEN, PRINCESS, MICHAEL, TOM, BIB, TUCKER, JANE, WAYNE, SHANE, (The last three in their own appalling version of court dress) PERI and the courtiers.

KING: That was a lovely dinner; all my favourites – game pie, roast pheasant, wild boar....

QUEEN: Known to the chef as roadkill ragout.

KING: And nothing to disturb the calm.

MICHAEL: I'm afraid that I must disturb the calm; I've a very important question to ask you.

KING: Ask away, young man, ask away! There's very little that could upset me.

MICHAEL: Very well; *(Pause.)* I wish for the Princess's hand in marriage. *(All appear stunned, apart from the PRINCESS who sees this as a very welcome development.)*

QUEEN: What?! Why, you cheeky thing; we hardly know you.

KING: This is a bit of a surprise – I shall have to think about it, although I don't have any major objection.

QUEEN: Well I do! He's too young!

PRINCESS: But we don't know how old he is.

QUEEN: He's too short!

KING: He's taller than me.

QUEEN: He's too tall!

BIB: And he's no sense of style.

TUCKER: Not like us.

PRINCESS: You're all just inventing reasons to say no! Don't any of you care about my happiness?

PERI: *(Stepping forward.)* I think that she has a point, Majesties; none of those are good reasons to say no.

JANE: And that's my best boy you're running down.

WAYNE: Can we run him down too?

SHANE: Preferably with a herd of buffalo. *(There is a clap of thunder, a flash of lightning and the lights dim; the OGRE and his imps burst in.)*

OGRE: There'll be no marriage! Except to me! The tables are well and truly turned! So much for your plans; it's <u>your</u> lands which will be seized, not mine, together with all your gold, jewels and this palace.

KING: I don't understand; whose plans?

OGRE: *(Pointing to them, one by one.)* The witch, that boy and his cat; they thought that their foolish little plot was a secret. But I'm no fool – I've known about it all along. I've won and you've lost – you'll all become my slaves!

JANE: Ooh! What a rude man; slaves indeed! My late hubbie tried that one on me, and much good it did him.

QUEEN: Peri! Why don't you do something? Put a spell on him; what's the point of having magic powers if you don't use them?

PERI: I hate to say it, but I'm powerless against him; he's too strong for my brand of magic to have any effect. My magic only works on humans and animals – and he's neither.

JANE: Well he smells like an animal – pooh! Are you sure that he isn't one?

OGRE: Quiet woman, before I turn you into the old bat you are. There's absolutely nothing any of you can do.

PERI: *(Aside to TOM.)* Oh yes, there is; do what you do best.

TOM: What, take <u>him</u> on? You must be joking!

PERI: *(Again aside.)* Not brawn, you footling feline! Use your brain and cunning.

TOM: *(The light dawns.)* Oh, I see! Leave it to me. *(Coming forward to face the OGRE.)* It seems that we have to accept defeat, oh mighty one.

OGRE: At last – a little respect. Very wise – but it won't help you.

TOM: Oh I know that, but before you and your creatures take us and all our possessions and make us slaves for ever, there's something I must know.

OGRE: I'm feeling generous, so I'm prepared to humour you before I have you turned into a rug. What is it that you must know?

TOM: I've been assured on the highest authority that you can turn yourself into any creature you want. But frankly, I find that hard to believe.

OGRE: *(Bristling.)* Believe it, for it is indeed true!

TOM: Isn't!

OGRE: Is!

ALL: Isn't!

OGRE: Is too! Foolish cat – I'll prove it!

There is a flash and blackout; the actor playing the OGRE is replaced by another, dressed as a lion or some other large, fierce animal. Their voices will need to be similar or the lines spoken from offstage. Everyone except TOM shrinks back.

OGRE: There! Told you so!

TOM: Very impressive. However, anyone can be big and fierce, but surely it would be much more difficult to be a small creature like a rat for instance or – a mouse! Even better. Then you could go where you want, seeing but unseen. Bet you can't do that!

OGRE: Of course I can!

TOM: Can't!

OGRE Can! Watch and be amazed!

There is another flash and blackout; the lion is replaced by a mouse, possibly clockwork or pulled across the stage on a string.

TOM: They fall for it every time! Goodbye and good riddance!

TOM pounces on the mouse and 'kills' it. Everyone cheers. When the imps realise what has happened they cower in their turn. The lights come up to full.

MICHAEL: Well done Tom! *(Embracing him.)* I knew you could do it.

TOM: *(Breaking away and dusting off his paws.)* Gerroff you great softie! Never doubted it; piece of cake.

PRINCESS: Oh, Tom! You've saved us! *(She kisses him; he looks startled but then preens.)* Mother! Father! You can't possibly object to our marriage now. The Marquis and his brave cat have saved the kingdom.

KING: I can't help thinking that they've nearly cost us the kingdom. But yes, I think that he's worthy and your mother does too, don't you dear?

QUEEN: For once I do, as he now appears to have inherited all the ogre's lands and treasures. All's well that ends well, I suppose. *(Everyone cheers.)*

JANE: Ooh, I'm so pleased; but we seem to have forgotten about these poor creatures. *(Indicating the imps.)* What shall we do with them?

PERI: I haven't forgotten them. They're safe now – out of the ogre's power. Now, let me see what I can do for them. I know! I'm up to my eyes in work – I could do with some apprentices. *(She makes a pass over the IMPS.)*

Up you get, no need to cower
Now you've escaped the ogre's power.
No longer will you do his bidding,
You're *my* slaves now. No, only kidding!

(The lights dim momentarily, changing colours; the IMPS get to their feet.) There, that's better! *(More cheers.)* Perhaps it's time you had a little love in your lives.

Song: possibly 'Love is all around', Wet, Wet, Wet – sung by Peri, joined by all.

IMPS: Thank you! Thank you!

MICHAEL: I second that; my good fortune is all down to you and Tom.

TOM: Recognition at last!

MICHAEL: And as soon as we can clear up the Ogre's castle, with the help of your apprentice imps, we'll have a party to celebrate.

PRINCESS: And everyone's invited! *(PERI turns to address the audience.)*

PERI: The ogre's plan's gone off the boil,
He's shuffled off his mortal coil.
So let's now raise our crowns and hats,
To our dear Tom – the king of cats!

Everyone cheers as the curtains close. The curtains open again for the walkdown, a reprise of songs used in the show and final bows.